Everyday
KINDNESS

Everyday KINDNESS

Spiritual Refreshment
for Women

Patricia Mitchell

BARBOUR
PUBLISHING

Contents

Introduction

In our busy world, practical acts of kindness that sweeten life, connect people, and strengthen relationships are rare. Yet there are still people—people like you—who believe that kindness is important. God has blessed you richly, and you're moved to respond by blessing the lives of others. As His Spirit continues to work in your heart, you desire to grow in love, kindness, and compassion for everyone.

Everyday Kindness is designed to bless you for all the times you have shown kindness to others and to help you discover more ways to live a life marked by God-pleasing, Spirit-empowered kindness. Yes, it's a busy world, but some people—including you—are never too busy to care about what's truly important in life. God bless you for being the kind and caring woman you are!

The Spirit produces the fruit of love,
joy, peace, patience, kindness.
GALATIANS 5:22 NCV

Ability

GIFT OF KINDNESS

Do not neglect the gift that is in you.
1 TIMOTHY 4:14 NKJV

We each have many abilities, and it's not all about how well we excelled in school or what level of proficiency we reached in music or sports. If that were the case, many of us would have to declare ourselves not able at all! But God says differently. He has granted everyone the gift of special abilities, and He intends for each of us to develop, share, and enjoy them. The more you use your skills and talents, the more you grow in appreciation for the great kindness God has shown to you, and the more you kindly share with others.

HE ENABLES YOU

I can do everything through Christ,
who gives me strength.
PHILIPPIANS 4:13 NLT

Despite your best intention to treat everyone kindly, emotions can get in the way. Stress, fatigue, and frustration can trigger sharp rebukes and angry replies that you later regret. When emotions threaten your ability to respond kindly to others, pause and let God's unfailing kindness embrace your heart and mind. Treat yourself kindly by receiving God's forgiveness and forgiving yourself. God restores your peace, enabling you to curb negative feelings and thwart unproductive emotions. The comfort God sends strengthens your confidence and increases your ability to pour out His kindness on others.

Action

THE PICTURE OF KINDNESS

*Let us not love with words or speech
but with actions and in truth.*

1 JOHN 3:18 NIV

"A picture is worth a thousand words" is certainly true as it pertains to kindness. All the kind, well-intentioned words and phrases in the world are meaningless unless they're backed up with objective, observable, and kind actions. But while kind words trip easily off the tongue, kind actions come at the cost of time, effort, and attention to the needs of others. It is God's action in your life that enables you not simply to speak kindly but to act kindly. With His Spirit as your counselor and guide, you are the picture of kindness!

A GOOD LIGHT

Everyone who lives by the truth will come to the light, because they want others to know that God is really the one doing what they do.
JOHN 3:21 CEV

Those who represent a company or a nation are expected to act a certain way. Whatever they say and do as individuals reflects back on the business or country, so they are careful to think before they speak and consider the consequences of their actions. Do you know that God has given you the privilege of representing Him to others? As a beloved daughter of your heavenly Father, your gentle words and kind, compassionate actions not only put you in a good light but put Him in a good light too.

Adversity

GOD'S HEART AND HANDS

Remember those who are suffering
as if you were suffering with them.
HEBREWS 13:3 NCV

"It's lonely at the top," say some high-level executives, diplomats, and policy makers. With no one but themselves accountable for decisions that affect hundreds if not millions of people, they carry a heavy burden. An equally lonely place, however, is at the opposite end of society—those who live in poverty-stricken areas, who have lost their source of income, who are bound by adversity, addiction, or mental illness. Alone and forgotten, they are in need of your compassion and kindness. It's your heart and your hands that God uses to ease the suffering of others.

A KINDLY RESPONSE

*We know that all things work
together for good to those who love God.*
ROMANS 8:28 NKJV

When adversity enters your life, you have every reason to feel that God isn't being very kind! You ask yourself why you should have to confront this issue or handle this problem. Why this hardship, when you've been doing all the right things? Yet God's wisdom reaches far beyond human understanding. If you are facing a difficult challenge right now, put your burden in God's care. Rely on Him to turn whatever you're going through to your ultimate advantage. Let Him shower you with His kindness and comfort, peace and hope.

Advice

KINDLY ADVISED

*Everyone enjoys a fitting reply; it is wonderful
to say the right thing at the right time!*
PROVERBS 15:23 NLT

When people ask for your advice, you've been given both a privilege and a burden. A privilege because they think highly of your experience and perspective, and they believe you can point them in the right direction. You've also received a burden, though, because what you say may influence their decisions and actions, so choose your words carefully. Good advice kindly given from mature Christians is one of the ways God guides His people when they're at a crossroads in life. Just as you have received the blessing of good advice, so your good advice is a blessing to others.

GODLY COUNSEL

*"I say these things so
that you may be saved."*
JOHN 5:34 ESV

During His earthly ministry, Jesus taught everyone who would listen about the things of God. Those who heard and heeded His advice received saving faith, spiritual wisdom, and the God-given ability to live a life of goodness and grace. But others walked away because they were uncomfortable with what He told them about sin, repentance, and salvation. It wasn't what they wanted to hear! Yet Jesus didn't stop telling the truth with great kindness. You follow His example when you bring His counsel—even His difficult counsel—to others with words of kindness and a heart of love.

Anger

A GOOD EXCHANGE

*If you are angry, you cannot do any
of the good things that God wants done.*
JAMES 1:20 CEV

How quickly anger gets out of control! What might start out as a natural reaction to offense, injury, or injustice can quickly flare into a craving for revenge, which leads to a never-ending cycle of punishing words and violent actions. Clearly, this isn't the way God wants you to handle angry feelings. Instead, He offers you the power and the wisdom to exchange anger for composure, retaliation for forgiveness, and cruelty for kindness. God wants these good things done, and His Spirit at work in your heart empowers you to accomplish them.

THREE KINDLY STEPS

Don't befriend angry people or associate with hot-tempered people, or you will learn to be like them.

PROVERBS 22:24–25 NLT

Anger is contagious. If someone has ever screamed at you in rage, you know how difficult it is to remain calm, much less respond with kindness and understanding. While it's not always possible to avoid people given to outbursts of anger, you can protect yourself in three ways: First, listen without commenting or contradicting. Second, respond in a gentle and kind voice, setting the tone for a productive conversation. Third, and most important, pray for them as you would for any hurting soul in need of God's comfort and love.

Attitude

A KIND COMPANION

*Let the Spirit renew your
thoughts and attitudes.*
EPHESIANS 4:23 NLT

When you start the day with a positive attitude, kindness is a natural response. Since you feel good about yourself, treat yourself kindly—no nit-picking your appearance or personality! As you put others in a positive light, compassion and understanding flow from your heart. You respond kindly to the people around you because that's the way you genuinely feel. Even in unpleasant situations, you pause to discover a blessing and thank God for it. Begin each day with a prayer for a positive attitude toward yourself, others, and your circumstances, and kindness will accompany you every step of the way.

THE ATTITUDE OF JESUS

May the God who gives endurance and encouragement give you the same attitude of mind toward each other that Christ Jesus had.
ROMANS 15:5 NIV

You don't have to delve far into the biblical account of Jesus' earthly ministry to discover how He treated people. Personifying God's attitude, Jesus extended incomparable kindness and overwhelming compassion. He saw people, not as a means to get what He wanted or as faceless beings in a crowd, but as individuals, each created in the image of God. Each with a God-given purpose. Each in need of His kindness. Through Him, your loving attitude toward others is a bright reflection of His loving attitude toward you.

Beauty

THE ROSE OF SHARON

I am a rose of Sharon, a lily of the valleys.
SONG OF SOLOMON 2:1 ESV

The Plain of Sharon lies between the Mediterranean Sea and the hills of modern-day Israel. While what the rose of Sharon looked like is uncertain, clearly the bride of Solomon who compared herself to an exquisite flower had confidence in her worth and beauty. Without a doubt her poise and self-assurance added to her attractiveness. These words are not recorded simply to laud the love of one couple, but to give you, in earthly terms, an idea of the love God has for you. As He showers His kindness on you, you are His beautiful, exquisite rose of Sharon forever.

UNCHANGING STYLE

*Charm is deceptive, and beauty
does not last; but a woman who fears
the LORD will be greatly praised.*
PROVERBS 31:30 NLT

If you enjoy paging through fashion magazines, you might notice that the standard of beauty changes constantly. Sultry exotic looks give way to down-home freshness. Tight, sexy jeans are succeeded by soft, billowy dresses. What's "in" today is "out" tomorrow! Mercifully, God's standard of beauty has not changed since time began, and will not change. Graciousness, kindness, generosity, and gentleness continue to please Him. A heart filled with patience, love, and joy never fails to receive His favor. The best thing of all? You don't need to buy a thing. The beauty that God gives is yours for the asking!

Belief

THE BLESSING OF LIFE

You made us a little lower than you yourself,
and you have crowned us with glory and honor.
Psalm 8:5 CEV

It's natural to treat yourself kindly when you believe that God formed you, gave you the breath of life, and has a purpose in mind for you. Convinced of this spiritual truth, you avoid habits or lifestyles that would compromise your physical or emotional well-being. Your confidence stems from knowing the power of His Spirit at work in you, even if you stumble or lose your way from time to time. It's your belief in the blessedness of every living creature that enables you to regard yourself and others with God-given kindness and love.

A TEST OF FAITH

Dear friends, don't be surprised or
shocked that you are going through
testing that is like walking through fire.
1 PETER 4:12 CEV

From time to time, every believer faces faith-challenging situations. Mostly they're little more than dismissive remarks. But sometimes questions about religion or spirituality challenge long-held views on the subject and make you question what you believe and why. For some of God's people, challenges to their faith pit them against entrenched authority and strict social norms. Perhaps you don't confront such extreme conditions, but the tests you face are challenges to your faith. Don't be surprised. It comes with the territory, and God will show you how to respond with kindness, respect, and certainty.

Blessing

EXTRAORDINARY BLESSINGS

*"He who is mighty has done great
things for me, and holy is His name."*
LUKE 1:49 NKJV

After the angel told Mary that she would bear the Promised One, the young woman went to visit her cousin. Elizabeth, though at an advanced age, was also blessed with the gift of a child. Together the women celebrated the extraordinary kindness God had shown to them. Today God still blesses in amazing ways, for nothing is impossible for Him. Is there a gift you've never asked Him for because it seems too much to expect? Go ahead and ask, never doubting that He will bless you, and bless marvelously, according to His good and gracious will.

BE BLESSED

In Christ, God has given us every
spiritual blessing in the heavenly world.
EPHESIANS 1:3 NCV

The best blessings of all are the spiritual kind. For example, God's blessing of faith makes it possible for you to believe in Him and grow in love for Him. His blessing of hope enables you to face the future with optimism and the expectation of eternal life in heaven. His blessings of gentleness, kindness, patience, and joy give you the ability to love others in response to the love He has shown you. God never withholds spiritual blessings but generously pours them out through the presence of His Spirit in your heart. Ask and be blessed!

Challenge

POSE A CHALLENGE

*Don't copy the behavior and customs of
this world, but let God transform you into a
new person by changing the way you think.*
ROMANS 12:2 NLT

Living according to God's commandments is certainly
a challenge! The views of others, their actions, values,
and ambitions can clash with those God's Spirit puts in
your heart. But as the world challenges you, why not
challenge the world? Though you might not receive
kindness or consideration for acting according to God's
guidance, respond with kindness and consideration to
those who challenge your beliefs and values. Speak to
them with gentleness, and answer their questions with
understanding. Let them challenge you, never letting
go of the challenge you present to them with your life
of gentleness, peace, and love.

IT'S A CHALLENGE!

*Instruct the wise, and they will be
even wiser. Teach the righteous,
and they will learn even more.*
PROVERBS 9:9 NLT

Over the last several decades, technology has advanced with unprecedented speed. It's often a challenge to keep up with all the changes! Spiritually, it's a challenge to keep up, but not because God changes. You do. Your capacity to understand the things of God increases as you experience His work in your life, and your understanding of how to apply His teachings grows as you mature in faith. The more you actively meet the challenges you face every day, the more you grow in all His spiritual gifts, including kindness and compassion for others.

Change

A NEW SEASON

To everything there is a season,
a time for every purpose under heaven.
ECCLESIASTES 3:1 NKJV

You know that summer is turning to fall when you feel the first chill breeze across your face. In the same way, you can tell that winter is yielding to spring as the air warms and skies brighten. An unwelcome and bitter life change, however, can happen instantly. Confusion and anger are natural responses yet can never bring back a season once passed. If change has left you reeling, be kind to yourself. Give yourself time to embrace your new reality with the courage your kind and compassionate God offers to you.

COLORS OF CHANGE

Jesus Christ is the same yesterday
and today and forever.
HEBREWS 13:8 ESV

Life is like a kaleidoscope, constantly changing! If it didn't change, how quickly you'd slip into a monochromatic pattern, never to have new experiences, meet new people, or welcome new babies into the world. Yet amid change, there's a yearning for certainty and stability. You want to know there's something you can hold on to now and always, regardless of where you are in your life. That's why God has given you His promise that He will never change. And because He never changes, you can meet the myriad colors of change with acceptance, kindness, and grace.

Character

A QUESTION OF CHARACTER

*"Each tree is recognized by its own fruit.
People do not pick figs from thornbushes,
or grapes from briers."*
LUKE 6:44 NIV

When you want to determine a person's character, you use your eyes. Regardless of what the person says about herself, you watch her actions. Do her choices correspond with her glowing self-assessment? Does she, for example, consider herself kind and generous yet act in ways that hurt and deprive others? If so, you've uncovered a serious character issue! For a quick check of your own character, examine your own actions. Shine a light on any gaps between opinion and fact, imagination and reality. Ask for God's help as you surely, steadily, and objectively grow in godly character.

THE CORE OF CHARACTER

Don't ever forget kindness and truth.
Wear them like a necklace. Write them
on your heart as if on a tablet.
PROVERBS 3:3 NCV

Truth and kindness form the core of godly character. When truth or kindness is set aside for gain or convenience, ambition or greed, godly character suffers and eventually crumbles. How does it happen? Little by little, with each white lie, unkind comment, and selfish decision. That's why God gives you this command: Don't ever forget truth and kindness! Practice kindness in real life, in real time. Speak the truth to real people, in real circumstances. Godly character increases the same way it weakens: bit by bit every day.

Choice

HE CHOSE YOU

*You did not choose me. I chose you
and sent you out to produce fruit,
the kind of fruit that will last.*

JOHN 15:16 CEV

During His earthly ministry, Jesus chose each of His disciples with a purpose in mind. They were not simply to talk about belonging to Him but to actually follow in His footsteps. Then as today, being chosen by the Lord calls for action! With great kindness He has chosen you by planting faith in your heart and stirring your desire to make your relationship with Him more tangible and real. Kindness to others is just one of many actions that show you belong to Him—just one of the many fruits that will last.

YOU CHOOSE HIM

*"Choose for yourselves this
day whom you will serve."*
JOSHUA 24:15 NKJV

Though God has chosen you to serve Him, He gives you the option to choose other gods and serve them with your time and energy. Many people do. They prefer to chase after fame, money, or status. They place their own thoughts, desires, and understanding above God's commandments and His revealed truth. Yet with unbounded kindness, God loves everyone and welcomes all who return to Him with a repentant heart. He forgives and comforts, and He once again asks the question: Whom will you serve? Choose for yourself.

Clear Thinking

A CLEAR MESSAGE

You need someone to teach you the elementary truths of God's word all over again.
HEBREWS 5:12 NIV

God has clearly declared His message of love for you in the words of scripture. Additionally, He has shown you His compassion for you through the ministry of His Son, Jesus. But questions, doubts, opinion, and speculation complicate beliefs, and erroneous teachings further muddle the mind. If your thinking about God and your relationship with Him is confused, go to the source: scripture. Read what God says. Talk with mature Christians whose Spirit-sent wisdom empowers them to speak the truth with clarity, kindness, and love.

A REASONABLE IDEA

"Come now, let us reason together, says the LORD."
ISAIAH 1:18 ESV

"Please listen to reason!" you might beg a friend whose view is clouded by wishful thinking, erroneous information, or preconceived opinions. Though it's a difficult conversation, you want to save her from making a serious mistake or embarking on an ill-advised path. Your heart of kindness obliges you to do what you can to influence your friend for the better. In the same way, God's heart of kindness compels Him to guide you through every season of your life. In love, He gives you His commandments and makes His will known so you can think clearly about spiritual things.

Comfort

COMPELLED TO COMFORT

He makes me to lie down in green pastures;
He leads me beside the still waters.
PSALM 23:2 NKJV

If you take care of children, you wouldn't willfully subject them to unnecessary stress. Instead, you would do everything possible to comfort them when they appeared anxious or fearful. Your love would compel you to treat them with nothing but abundant kindness. Similarly, God's love compels Him to pour His abundant kindness on you. Even when necessity dictates correction, His Spirit leads you to the comfort of forgiveness, compassion, restoration, and reconciliation. His love never fails! With kindness beyond measure, He comforts your soul with His peace.

SURROUNDED WITH COMFORT

"They are blessed who grieve,
for God will comfort them."
MATTHEW 5:4 NCV

Among the many kindnesses God showers on you is the kindness of comfort. When disappointment leaves you feeling discouraged, your knowledge that God has a purpose for you gives you hope. When the loss of a loved one throws you into despair, your faith in His promise of eternal life gives you peace. When fear has you trembling, your trust in His control over all things provides your courage and confidence. God comforts you in many ways, and He enables you to comfort others with the same generosity and kindheartedness.

Commitment

NO MIDDLE ROAD

"You cannot serve God and money."
MATTHEW 6:24 ESV

"Stand in the middle of the road," someone once quipped, "and you'll get hit from both directions!" Those who would like to please God and please the world run the same risk. From God's side, there's His will for your life that you can't follow unless you commit yourself to His way. From the world's side, there are callous attitudes and mean-spirited behaviors you can't adopt unless you give up your relationship with God and ignore your spiritual yearnings. Only commitment to one side or the other gets you out of the middle of the road.

GENUINE COMMITMENT

Jesus Christ laid down his life for us.
1 JOHN 3:16 NIV

God chose to reveal His commitment to you by sending His Son, Jesus, into the world. In His life and ministry, Jesus demonstrated God's kindly feelings toward you and His desire to heal and comfort you, lead and guide you. Through His death on the cross, Jesus proved there's not one thing—even His life!—that He would not give for you. And because of His resurrection, you know He has the power to restore you too and grant you eternal life with Him. He's completely committed to you! All He asks is your genuine commitment to Him.

Compassion

FROM DEATH TO LIFE

Jesus said, "Neither do I condemn you;
go, and from now on sin no more."
<small>JOHN 8:11 ESV</small>

The biblical account of the woman caught in the act of adultery reveals Jesus' compassion to all who do wrong. Yes, the woman broke both the law of God and the law of the land. Consequences for her? Both spiritual and physical death. Yet the Lord did not condemn her; instead He admonished those who imagined themselves blameless. He did not send the woman away ashamed, but forgiven, renewed, restored, and strengthened. Today, He treats all who come to Him in repentance with the same life-giving kindness, compassion, and love.

COMPASSION AT WORK

*Encourage anyone who feels left out, help all
who are weak, and be patient with everyone.*
1 THESSALONIANS 5:14 CEV

True compassion gets busy. Imagine a friend of yours
is going through a tough time. Rather than avoid her
company, you seek it out. Because you feel compassion,
you listen and understand, encourage and comfort.
That's compassion at work! When you take the time to
make someone's way easier, assist a person less able
than yourself, and remember those who are suffering,
you are responding to the compassion God shows
toward you. With your kindness in action, you are
doing nothing less than demonstrating God's love for
all the world.

Confidence

CONFIDENCE IN HIM

If you think you are standing strong,
be careful not to fall.
1 CORINTHIANS 10:12 NLT

Perhaps at one time you put your confidence in a person, job, talent, or ambition that later failed you. Though sure of yourself at first, you later came to realize that you had planted the roots of your trust in sandy soil. It completely washed away under an onslaught of changing moods, events, and circumstances. Your confidence, if not planted firmly in God's grace and the Holy Spirit's power to nurture and cultivate it, lies on equally unstable ground. Make sure your confidence is planted, not in yourself or in other people or in any earthly structure, but in Him.

GOD-BASED CONFIDENCE

The LORD is on my side; I will not fear.
What can man do to me?
PSALM 118:6 ESV

A woman who lacks confidence in herself is seldom warm and inviting. She feels weak and vulnerable, often masking her inner fears with a tough outward manner. With your self-confidence built on God's love for you, however, you are free to show every kindness to others, even to those who aren't kind to you. You're willing to make yourself vulnerable, because God is your defense against anyone who would do you harm. When He is the source of your self-confidence, you can meet others with the tenderness and grace of a kind and gentle-hearted person.

Contentment

ENOUGH!

I say it is better to be content with what little you have. Otherwise, you will always be struggling for more, and that is like chasing the wind.

ECCLESIASTES 4:6 NCV

Have you ever said to yourself, "As soon as I get this or that, then I'll be content"? As soon as you had it in your possession, though, something else appeared on the horizon. So now another need came between you and contentment! The struggle to get more and more things leaves little heart-space for spiritual possessions like selflessness, compassion, kindness, peace, and joy. All those God-given gifts come your way when you say "enough." That one word empties your heart to receive the untold riches of true contentment.

LIFE IS GOOD

I have learned to be content
whatever the circumstances.
PHILIPPIANS 4:11 NIV

Is contentment always possible? With your faith placed firmly in God, the answer is *Yes*. Even if your circumstances are less than ideal right now, you know that the Lord stands beside you to strengthen and encourage you. You can rely on Him to provide the help you need and to show you the way through your difficulties. Leaning on Him, you receive the insight and courage it takes to change what you can for the better. Yes, today you are content with everything your kind, compassionate, purposeful God has placed on your path. Life is good, whatever the circumstances.

Courage

COURAGE FOR KINDNESS

Don't worry about what you will suffer.
REVELATION 2:10 CEV

It takes courage to be kind. That's because you are up against two formidable forces: the world's mockery and your human inclinations. First, your benevolent attitude and actions may breed jealousy in the hearts of those who consider themselves kind, but aren't. You open yourself to some very unfriendly criticism! Second, your humanity bends in toward itself, so kindness is not natural. Through God's Spirit dwelling in you, however, you're able to overcome selfishness by allowing Him to rule your life. Kindness takes courage, and because of Him, you have the courage that kindness requires.

DISAPPEARING DRAGONS

The LORD is my light and my salvation—
so why should I be afraid?
PSALM 27:1 NLT

Though dragons lurking under your bed at night have long since vanished, there are still things that cause you fear. Job loss, financial hardship, and broken relationships are only a few fire-breathing beasts with the power to send shivers down anyone's spine. God, as a caring parent rushes in to calm a frightened child, moves to calm your heart. His words soothe you, His love embraces you, and His presence assures you that He is still in control. The light of His love scatters the shadows, and you no longer fear. As your courage grows, your worries disappear.

Criticism

A DIFFICULT SUBJECT

We will speak the truth in love, growing in every way more and more like Christ.
EPHESIANS 4:15 NLT

Out of care and concern for someone, you may find yourself forced to open a difficult conversation. You know the person doesn't want to hear what you have to say, but you must say it because it affects physical, emotional, or spiritual health, or personal safety and well-being. Ask yourself: Is it true? Is it necessary? Is it kind? If you can answer "yes" to these three questions, you have a God-given duty to speak. Prepare your lips with a prayer that God will enable you to tell a difficult truth in the kindest way possible.

ON THE RIGHT PATH

Give a kind and respectful answer and keep
your conscience clear. This way you will make
people ashamed for saying bad things about
your good conduct as a follower of Christ.
1 PETER 3:16 CEV

When you choose to walk carefully on God's path instead of skipping along the most popular one, you're sure to hear some criticism. Some comments to reach your ears will sting, and possible disapproval from those close to you will hurt you deeply. But God's path allows for no condemnation in return, but only loving, respectful responses to their critical remarks. The knowledge that you are going forward as God's will would have you shields you from the shadows of shame, anger, and discouragement along the way.

Daily Walk

LITTLE THINGS MATTER

*"Whoever can be trusted with very
little can also be trusted with much."*
LUKE 16:10 NIV

Most days are filled not with larger-than-life opportunities to show how kind you are but with little
chances. With each friendly smile, welcoming word,
and helping hand, you are proving yourself a devoted
follower of God. Your small kindnesses become
known to all, and your thoughtful ways illustrate how
to walk with God each day, consistently and faithfully.
Yes, all those little kindnesses you have done and
continue to do matter tremendously, because later you
may discover that they've been the most important
things of all.

THE WAY IS MARKED

All the paths of the LORD
are mercy and truth.
PSALM 25:10 NKJV

Just as a walking path through the woods is discernible by the footsteps that went before, so God's path through life is marked for you. You see the footprints of believers ahead of you who remained faithful despite the challenges they confronted and the derision they suffered. The true and godly path through life's complexities is evident in the example of mature Christians who speak the truth in love, forgive others with generosity, and seek justice for everyone. There's little doubt you're on God's path when your daily walk is marked with acts of compassion, kindness, and caring.

Decisions

PRACTICAL DECISIONS

The disciples, as each one was able,
decided to provide help for the
brothers and sisters living in Judea.
ACTS 11:29 NIV

In the early church, believers in Syria learned of a severe famine sweeping through Jerusalem and the surrounding area. Scarce commodities had sent food prices soaring! Surely many powerful people in Syria knew about the famine, but the Syrian congregation decided to do something about it: They gave of their own resources so others could eat. When you decide to contribute practical aid to people in need, whether to help a suffering neighbor or relieve victims across the globe, your kindness is showing in the most practical way possible.

A SERIOUS MATTER

We make our own decisions, but the
Lord alone determines what happens.
PROVERBS 16:33 CEV

When it comes time to make serious decisions, you gather as much relevant information as you can, perhaps including the advice of experts. But you've probably learned that current facts and expert opinion alone aren't the whole story. There's intuition—what some might call a *gut feeling*. God's Spirit nudges you toward the way God would have you turn, even if your decision seems odd or unexpected to others. That's because reason doesn't always point to the kindest and most compassionate route to take, but God does. When you take Him seriously, He's a part of every decision you make.

Desires

SWEET DESIRE

A desire accomplished is sweet to the soul.
PROVERBS 13:19 NKJV

What's your heart's desire? Almost all worthwhile desires take time to accomplish. While you want to enjoy the journey, there's nothing like the feeling of having arrived! You can look back on perhaps years of work and dedication with justified pride and a heart of thanksgiving to God, who has blessed your efforts. Whether you are still reaching for your star or basking in its glow, God showers you with the kindness of people who encourage you, support you, and help you along. Whose heart's desire could you bless with that kind of godly goodness today?

FIRST IN HIS EYES

*"Anyone who wants to be first must
be the very last, and the servant of all."*
MARK 9:35 NIV

Most people like being first—first in line, first at the table, first to know. But being first often means pushing others out of the way, insisting on pride of place, and even ignoring the just claim of someone else. For the serious wannabe, kindness isn't an option! But Jesus tells you how to become first in His eyes: Desire to be last. Promote others ahead of yourself. Help them succeed in their plans and objectives. While humbly speaking of yourself, sing the praises of others. Wherever something needs to be done, be the first to do it.

Doubts

NOT SEEING, BUT BELIEVING

*"Blessed are those who have
not seen and yet have believed."*
JOHN 20:29 ESV

You've heard of doubting Thomas—he's the disciple who insisted on seeing the resurrected Lord before he'd believe Jesus lived. Instead of reprimanding Thomas, however, Jesus invited him to not only look but touch and feel Him too! This is the same way He responds to the doubts you may have about Him and His promises to you. You will hear no angry reproof, but only the gentle stirring of His Spirit in your heart working to strengthen your faith so you, though you haven't seen, may believe.

SOLID GROUND

Anyone who doubts is like an ocean
wave tossed around in a storm.
JAMES 1:6 CEV

In practical as well as spiritual matters, doubt puts you on shaky soil! It undermines growth, progress, and satisfaction. For example, if you doubt God's presence in your life, anxiety and fear keep you from living freely and joyfully. If you doubt yourself, lack of confidence makes you afraid to embrace new ideas, experiences, and relationships—the things that bring fulfillment to your life. Do you doubt God? Yourself? Today, take all your doubts to Him in prayer, trusting in His kindness and compassion. Let Him put you back on solid ground.

OVERWHELMING EMOTION

Whoever has no rule over his own spirit
is like a city broken down, without walls.
PROVERBS 25:28 NKJV

Emotions are strong and powerful. If you depend on your own strength of will or moral integrity to take you through the temptations that come into your life, watch out! While reason and determination can help you resist enticement, your emotions can deceive you. While your head whispers one thing, your heart shouts another. God knows both the power and the strength of human emotion, and He knows where feelings can carry you. Have you been there? Come, let Him embrace you in His forgiveness, comfort, and kindness. His overwhelming emotion toward you is love.

THE BLESSING OF EMOTION

*I praise you, for I am fearfully
and wonderfully made.*
PSALM 139:14 ESV

Emotions are one of God's many gifts. Used as He intended, emotions sweeten and strengthen bonds of family, friendship, marriage, and community. They make it possible for you to enjoy good times, feel the warmth of friendship and affection, laugh, love, and relive memories you'll cherish forever. Emotions enliven the present and fill the future with hopes, dreams, and exciting expectations. How long has it been since you have thanked God for His kindness to you in the stirrings of your emotions? Indeed, you are fearfully and wonderfully made!

Empathy

THE ULTIMATE KINDNESS

Rejoice with those who rejoice,
and weep with those who weep.
ROMANS 12:15 NKJV

If a friend's great joy has ever made you forget your troubles, or another person's dire predicament has ever made you put aside your plans, you have empathy for others. When others have something to celebrate, you celebrate with them. When they are stricken with sorrow, you listen to them, cry with them, and comfort them. At that moment, you are one with them in feeling, in understanding, in empathy. It's no wonder that empathy might well stand as the ultimate kindness you can give to another human soul.

KINDNESS PERSONIFIED

Though the LORD is supreme,
he takes care of those who are humble.
PSALM 138:6 NCV

"God's in His heaven," the poet Robert Browning exclaimed. "All's right with the world!" Certainly God is in His heaven, but He's also right here on Earth and right here with you. Rather than holding Himself far above the creatures He created, He moves among all people, understanding their concerns and caring about their troubles. In short, He empathizes. God sent His Son, Jesus, to show just how much He identifies with your sorrows, your burdens, and your cares. That's empathy carried to heavenly heights! That's kindness personified.

Encouragement

SIMPLE WORDS

Strengthen those who have tired hands,
and encourage those who have weak knees.
ISAIAH 35:3 NLT

A simple word of encouragement or act of kindness can live in memory for years and even a lifetime. You may think someone who holds a high position or appears to have everything under control doesn't need any encouragement, but you never know how unsure of herself or emotionally frayed she's feeling inside. Perhaps your "Wonderful job!" is the confidence booster she's longing to hear. It's possible your thumbs-up is all it will take for someone to know that others notice, understand, and care.

TIME OUT FOR ENCOURAGEMENT

*"Do all that is in your heart,
for the Lord is with you."*
2 Samuel 7:3 nkjv

Every day, why not encourage yourself? Take a few moments to fill your thoughts with gentle words of assurance and affirmation. Reflect on God's many kindnesses toward you in the past, and visualize the good plans He has for you right now. If you're lacking energy or feeling unappreciated, let Him whisper words of assurance in your heart. No, it's not just a trick to get yourself pumped for the duties of the day, but the way God renews a tired spirit, boosts sagging confidence, heightens appreciation for the present hour, and restores genuine enthusiasm.

Example

A GOOD WARNING

These things happened as a warning to us,
so that we would not crave evil things as they did.
1 CORINTHIANS 10:6 NLT

Someone once noted that those who refuse to set a good example serve as a dire warning for everyone else. It's true! Words of caution may come across as old-fashioned and dull, but one person's downfall brings those words to life, often quite dramatically. A bad example serves as a warning to the wise. When you examine your own behavior, measure it against God's wise counsel, which is designed to keep you safe. The good example you set doing kind and thoughtful things is a blessing to those who would follow you.

A GODLY EXAMPLE

Always set a good example for others.
TITUS 2:7 CEV

Whenever you're out among people, your words and conduct, appearance and attitude are on display. If they like what they see, they want to know you better. They might even ask you the secret of your serenity, confidence, kindness, and joy. What a perfect time to tell them about your faith in God and your trust in His protection and care! They will listen when you say that your example is Jesus Christ, because your actions back up your words. By setting a godly example, you open the ears of others to the voice of God's kindness and love.

Excellence

THE HIGHEST PATH

*Supplement your faith with a generous provision
of moral excellence, and moral excellence with
knowledge, and knowledge with self-control,
and self-control with patient endurance,
and patient endurance with godliness.*
2 PETER 1:5–6 NLT

It all starts with saving faith in Jesus Christ. Faith in Him prompts you to learn more about who God is and what He desires of you, so you search His Word, increasing your knowledge and understanding of His precepts. With the help of His Spirit at work in you, you pursue moral excellence through self-control and the curbing of unkind feelings, thoughts, and actions. These things aren't part of your life anymore, because in Him you have chosen the highest, most excellent path.

THE KEY TO EXCELLENCE

"Many women have done excellently,
but you surpass them all."
PROVERBS 31:29 ESV

Kindhearted people are everywhere! There's the stranger in a distant place you visited who not only directed you where you wanted to go but also went out of her way to make sure you arrived safely. And how about the compassionate professional who put in extra time and effort to help when your family was stricken by a devastating loss? For sure, kindness is not the sole province of professed believers, but of people everywhere. Yet you know God and believe in Him. In His eyes, you not only do very well but also exceed them all.

Expectation

MEETING HIS EXPECTATIONS

*"From everyone who has been given much,
much will be demanded. And from the one
trusted with much, much more will be expected."*
LUKE 12:48 NCV

A teacher provides detailed instructions, answers questions, and then gives her students a test. She expects good results! In the same way, God expects good results from the knowledge and understanding you have of Him and His will. He continues to instruct you through the words of scripture, the example of mature Christians, and the action of His Spirit in your heart. He's looking for thoughtfulness, kindness, and compassion from you. Yes, there will be tests along the way, but you're on track to meet His expectations as you faithfully follow the guidelines He gives you.

IT'S A PROMISE

"You will grieve, but your
grief will turn to joy."
JOHN 16:20 NIV

When God makes a promise in scripture, you can expect Him to fulfill it. One of His many promises provides special comfort when you're grieving for any reason—loss of someone special, of health, of hope, of livelihood. Throughout the darkest hours of sorrow, He is there in His kindness to hold you in His arms, dry your tears, and soothe the wounds of your soul. At times like these, it's hard to imagine that things could ever get better, but they will. You can expect it because He has promised.

Family

SISTER IN CHRIST

*"Anyone who does God's will is
my brother and sister and mother."*
MARK 3:35 NLT

Where humanity draws boundaries between nations
and highlights differences between people, God gathers
together into one family all those who believe in Him.
Whether your earthly family numbers few or many,
your spiritual family includes all who know Jesus as
their Lord and Savior. Imagine! You are a sister in Christ
with all believers of the past, present, and future! As
He has extended His great kindness to you, let your
heart pour out kindness on all, especially those who
belong to your family of faith.

FAMILY UNITY

Whoever troubles his own household will inherit the wind.
PROVERBS 11:29 ESV

When disharmony, struggle, and conflict enter a home, family life becomes unbearable. If bitterness or discontent has a place at the table, there is no peace in the house, even for people who live alone. It's time to open the door wide and invite God inside. Selfishness slips away with the knowledge that He will provide for everyone's needs, and dissention disappears when all things are submitted to His will. Peace comes to your home as respect produces unity, kindness rules behavior, and love infuses relationships, especially the relationship you have with yourself.

Finance

A PLACE FOR MONEY

*Don't worry and ask yourselves, "Will we
have anything to eat? Will we have anything
to drink? Will we have any clothes to wear?"*
Matthew 6:31 cev

Everyone needs money! Without money, you would
have no means of putting food on the table, clothes on
your back, and a roof over your head. Money enables
you to provide for your well-being and the well-being
of others. There's trouble, however, if money becomes
your sole focus, either because you rely on your wealth
for your security and happiness or because you fret over
making ends meet rather than rely on God's power to
provide. Treat money as the blessing that God intends,
and money will treat you kindly too.

MONEY PROBLEMS? GONE!

Command them to do good, to be rich in good deeds,
and to be generous and willing to share.
1 Timothy 6:18 niv

No matter how much or how little you have in your bank account, God invites you to share with others. Sharing is a privilege He offers to everyone, because He knows that a healthy and wholesome relationship with money depends on it. Just ask someone who gives generously of her financial resources to help others and support God's work. You'll discover that the source of her joy and contentment and her sense of purpose and satisfaction with life rest in her willingness to be used by God. Share in proportion to the blessings God has given to you, and your financial problems will dwindle.

Forgiveness

EVEN THAT ONE

As far as the east is from the west, so far
has He removed our transgressions from us.
PSALM 103:12 NKJV

Perhaps there is something that burdens your heart—a word you would give anything to take back, or an act you have never confessed to anyone. Though you know God forgives, you doubt He could forgive the particular transgression you're thinking about right now. Yet with overwhelming kindness and compassion, God reaches out to you. He pleads with you to let go of that burden and anything else weighing on your heart. The death and resurrection of His Son, Jesus Christ, has removed your guilt, and all your sins are completely forgiven. Yes, even that one.

MEASURE FOR MEASURE

*Be kind and loving to each other, and forgive
each other just as God forgave you in Christ.*
Ephesians 4:32 NCV

You show great kindness to the person you forgive
from the heart. And in forgiving, you're also showing
great kindness to yourself. No longer will you harbor
anger against the person and allow resentment to sour
your outlook on life. The thought of a past offense
won't dampen your happiness today, and the burden
of bitterness won't drag down your relationships
with others and with God. See, God has given you an
example: He has forgiven you completely and without reservation. Forgive with the same measure of
kindness, and you receive forgiveness in return.

Friendship

FRIENDS FOREVER

*"I have called you friends, for everything
that I learned from my Father I
have made known to you."*
JOHN 15:15 NIV

God may have blessed you with a few close friends. You can talk to them about anything and you love spending time with them. Not only do they know you well, but they also sometimes seem to know you better than you know yourself! Even more of a blessing, however, is the friend you have in Jesus. No matter who may come or go in your life, Jesus' presence remains. He invites you to talk to Him in prayer. He extends His comfort and counsel to you in scripture. The kindness of His friendship is something you can depend on forever.

A FRIEND TO CHERISH

If one falls down,
the other can help him up.
ECCLESIASTES 4:10 NCV

You enjoy the company of someone new, but only with time can you know if this is the beginning of a long-lasting friendship. You will see evidence of friendship if she cares about your thoughts and feelings and responds supportively to the events in your life. You will know too in your own eagerness to give her your time and attention, and your willingness to do everything you can to encourage her. If these marks are evident, you have in each other a source of help and affirmation, kindness and love. God has blessed you with a friend to cherish.

Fruitfulness

FROM INSIDE OUT

The gospel is bearing fruit and growing
throughout the whole world—just as it has
been doing among you since the day you heard it.
COLOSSIANS 1:6 NIV

Once you hear and believe that God truly loves you, God's Spirit goes to work deep inside your heart. You receive a sense of self-confidence and self-esteem because you realize how much you're worth in God's eyes. At peace with yourself, you desire to extend God's love to others, for now you can recognize His presence in them. You become a kinder and gentler person, more understanding, thoughtful, and respectful, even among those who test your patience. From the inside out, your fruitfulness grows—and shows.

GOOD ROOTS

"I am the vine; you are the branches.
Those who remain in me, and I
in them, will produce much fruit."
JOHN 15:5 NLT

Plants with beautiful blooms and trees with sweet, tasty fruit require a strong and healthy root system. Without it, you have nothing but bare stalks. In the same way, God-pleasing acts of generosity, thoughtfulness, and kindness result only when His Spirit has planted, nourished, and cultivated the seed of faith. Genuine joy and long-lasting peace of mind are not possible unless your heart is firmly established in Him. And when it is, kindness blossoms naturally and abundantly in all the things you think, say, and do.

Future

CLEAR GOALS

You should say, "If the Lord wants,
we will live and do this or that."
JAMES 4:15 NCV

It's exciting to have goals for the future. Having a clear destination gives your life's journey direction and purpose. But sometimes you run up against a detour or even a roadblock, and you're left bewildered, wondering what to do next. Ask God! Perhaps He wants to point out another path for you to take before you reach your goal, or maybe He has a new and better destination in mind for you. Or it could be He simply wants you to take it a little slower. Yes, work toward your goals, but leave the future entirely in God's hands.

NO WORRIES

"Do not worry about tomorrow,
for tomorrow will worry about its own things."
MATTHEW 6:34 NKJV

"If you see ten troubles coming down the road," Calvin Coolidge remarked, "you can be sure that nine will run into the ditch before they reach you." And for the one trouble that might reach you, worrying about it beforehand won't help at all! God gives you each day minute by minute, hour by hour. Why waste a moment of it fretting over what God, in His wisdom, is withholding until tomorrow? In loving kindness, He frees you to live deeply and love completely the present hour. Trust in Him to do the same with each new tomorrow.

Gentleness

STRENGTH IN GENTLENESS

*"Bless those who curse you,
pray for those who mistreat you."*
LUKE 6:28 NIV

What does it take to respond gently to a spiteful comment, hurtful insult, belligerent challenge, or hostile remark? Certainly not human weakness, but heavenly strength. Only a strong commitment to God's divine command to bless others restrains a natural impulse to meet hurt with hatred. It takes strength of character tested and honed in real-life situations to return gentleness for harshness, kindness for cruelty. In the face of offense, there's no response that makes you stronger or leaves you stronger than gentleness.

YOU NEVER KNOW

Always be gentle with others.
PHILIPPIANS 4:5 CEV

You never know what others are going through. Though you may see nothing but the faces of ordinary men and women on the outside, inside there are hearts burdened with intractable problems, terrible disappointments, devastating regrets, and overwhelming grief. It could be the warmth of your smile that lifts a heart today, and the kindness of your thoughtful gesture that shines a ray of brightness into someone's gloom. God may use your friendly words or your willingness to listen to give hope, faith, and courage to a despairing heart. Always be gentle with others, because you never know.

Giving

WHAT YOU GIVE

Whoever sows sparingly will also
reap sparingly, and whoever sows
bountifully will also reap bountifully.
2 CORINTHIANS 9:6 ESV

The more you give, the more you get in return. When you give your work your best effort, you get more satisfaction out of your day. When you give your full attention to those around you, you get better relationships, and when you give kindness, compassion, and understanding to others, you most often get the same in return. When you give a portion of each day to meditation, prayer, and spiritual reading, you get the best of all—a strong, vibrant, and growing friendship with God.

LOVE IS THE REASON

"Freely you have received; freely give."
MATTHEW 10:8 NIV

God gave you everything you have—your life and breath, abilities and talents, opportunities and experiences, memories of yesterday and hopes for the future. All this purely out of love for you! No price tag attached. All He asks is for you to be thankful, cherish His good gifts, and share them with others. Give freely and generously. Take time for kindnesses both big and small. Use your talents to brighten the life of someone else. Share a portion of your material resources with those who have less than you do for no other reason than love.

Golden Rule

ECHO OF KINDNESS

*"Whatever you wish that others
would do to you, do also to them."*
MATTHEW 7:12 ESV

The Golden Rule sums up Jesus' teaching about relationships. He treated the people around Him with compassion and understanding, and in so doing, He set the example for anyone who would follow in His way. If you desire warmth, friendliness, and consideration, don't wait for those things; do them. If you would like people to behave with more respect and gentleness, show them how with your own respect and gentleness. You will be surprised how often you will get in return the blessing you extend to others. Like an echo, kindness comes back to you.

THIS IS HOW

*"He is kind even to people
who are ungrateful."*
LUKE 6:35 NCV

What about the times you make every effort to be friendly, but you're rebuffed? It happens! Even Jesus in His earthly ministry experienced the sting of rejection. Yet the Golden Rule still applies. Even though someone doesn't respond with kindness to you, God still invites you, and enables you, to live up to His Golden Rule. Look at it this way—not always have you responded to His generous overtures, but He in no way gave up His kind thoughts toward you. God, in His never-changing love, shows you how to obey the Golden Rule.

Goodness

WHAT GOODNESS!

*Every good gift and every
perfect gift is from above.*
JAMES 1:17 ESV

As you apply God's guidelines to your daily conduct and interactions with people, don't be surprised if you get a reputation for being a good person. What a compliment! It means that people know you care about their needs and will help them in real and practical ways. They look to you for thoughtful advice and trust your judgment. People let down their guard around you because your kindness has never let them down. All this stems from the goodness of God, who has showered His goodness on you.

GODLY GOODNESS

"He gives his sunlight to both the evil and the good, and he sends rain on the just and the unjust alike."
MATTHEW 5:45 NLT

Certainly you have no problem being good to those who are good to you. But you might have a problem with people who aren't very nice, who don't show you kindness, or who ignore your presence. It's hard to be good to them! Yet this is precisely what God would have you do. When you meet them, greet them with warmth and friendliness. If an opportunity arises, do them a favor. You may find, under their shell of distrust, a gentle soul yearning for your friendship. But even if you don't, you have been good—just like God.

Grace

INFINITE KINDNESS

You have been saved by grace through believing.
You did not save yourselves; it was a gift from God.
EPHESIANS 2:8 NCV

Imagine for a moment if your entrance to heaven depended on how many good things you did. No matter how stellar your behavior, how much you help others, and how awesome your accomplishments, this question would haunt your days: Are you doing enough to please God? That's why God, in His infinite kindness, has lifted that burden off your shoulders. It's called grace. He poured out His grace on you as a gift so you can rest assured of His love and your place in heaven with Him forever.

ALWAYS GRACE

May God's grace be eternally upon
all who love our Lord Jesus Christ.
Ephesians 6:24 nlt

What individuals deserve or don't deserve might enter human thoughts, but not God's thoughts. The question of whether you deserve His grace, for example, doesn't cross His mind as He showers you with His mercy, forgiveness, and the reassurance of His love. Though even great trespasses may weigh the soul, His grace never fails to comfort. Despite repeated stumbles along the way, His grace always lifts up, gives strength, and provides hope for another day. There's one thing you can depend on, and that's God's grace in every time of need.

Guidance

HIS HAND OF KINDNESS

Correct me, LORD, but please be gentle.
JEREMIAH 10:24 NLT

God guides with two hands. One hand holds up His rules, the *dos* and *don'ts* designed to keep you close to Him and protect you from the many pitfalls of life. His other hand, however, remains free to lift up those who stumble along the way. Through human weakness and poor choices, you may trip over His laws; when that happens, remember God's willingness to forgive. He'll pick you up, dust you off, and put you back on His path. No matter how many times you fall, He continues to guide you with gentleness and kindness, forgiveness and love.

KINDLY GUIDANCE

Parents, don't be hard on your children.
If you are, they might give up.
COLOSSIANS 3:21 CEV

Even if you don't have young children at home or supervise people in the workplace, you still guide others. People hear your words and tone of voice when you speak, and they gladly listen or angrily turn away. They see what you do, and your behavior leads them to respect you or distrust you. And if you are in a position to offer advice or deliver instructions, here's the kind and effective way of doing it. Speak respectfully, act honorably, and guide others with kindness, just as God guides you.

Happiness

SCAM ALERT

Happy is the person who trusts the LORD,
who doesn't turn to those who are proud.
PSALM 40:4 NCV

Be careful! Emails that promise you millions of dollars if you wire a certain amount of up-front money don't deliver on their promise. They're called *scams* for good reason! Similarly, many things that promise happiness—fame, status, wealth, and popularity—are like scams. They lure you with appealing claims, but they don't deliver. Let God, whose promises never fail, show you where true happiness lies. Allow His Spirit to create the inner qualities that create a happy life, qualities like earned confidence and self-esteem, constant kindness toward others, a positive outlook, godly ambitions, and complete contentment. He'll deliver!

HAPPY DAY

For the happy heart,
life is a continual feast.
PROVERBS 15:15 NLT

Happy people lift your spirits, make you smile, and leave you feeling good all day long. While they may have been born with a sunny disposition, it's more likely that at some point, they simply opted for happiness. It starts with a conscious choice to count blessings and cultivate gratitude, and then it seems there's no end of things to be happy about. When you catch yourself frowning at life, choose better for yourself and everyone around you. Offer God a "Thank You!" for the blessings all around you, and see how quickly you can have a happy day!

Health

CHERISH THE GIFT

You formed my inward parts;
You covered me in my mother's womb.
PSALM 139:13 NKJV

You have several reasons to keep your body as healthy and as fit as you can. First, the healthier you are, the better you'll feel about yourself. Second, good health enables your body to defend itself against infection, colds and flu, and other illnesses. Third, proper nutrition and exercise give you energy and uplift your mood. Yet the chief reason you want to avoid anything that would endanger your health is this one: Your body is a gift from God. Cherish the gift He has given to you by treating your body kindly. Take care of your health.

HE'LL DO THE REST

*"Your eye is the lamp of your body. When your eyes
are healthy, your whole body also is full of light."*
LUKE 11:34 NIV

Even more important than your physical health is your spiritual health. If you neglect to feed your soul with God's teachings, you will soon weaken in faith and in your dedication to His way. Letting your heart and mind fill with anger, bitterness, or discontent injures your outlook and perspective on life. Instead, actively and effectively nurture your spiritual health. Read and meditate on God's Word, nourish God-pleasing thoughts, and practice kindness and compassion toward others. Do everything you can, and then He will take care of the rest.

Help

HELP TO RESIST

Resist the devil and he will flee from you.
JAMES 4:7 NKJV

Jesus, during His earthly ministry, faced temptations designed to draw Him away from His Father's will. Though He was able to respond to each one with a resounding "No!" He was well aware that human weakness makes resisting temptation almost impossible at times. That's why He tenderly invites you to come to Him when temptations are luring you away from God's path. Ask Him to help you stand firm against sin. No matter how many times the same temptation may pull at your heart and soul, God's help to resist is only a prayer away.

SEND HELP!

"Call on me in the day of trouble;
I will deliver you, and you will honor me."
PSALM 50:15 NIV

By all means, ask God to help you with your problems; just don't tell Him how to do it! God in His great kindness sends help in many ways, and you wouldn't want to miss His answer because you were looking for your own solution. Instead, keep your eyes open for the direction you may not have considered and the opening you didn't previously see. Listen to the counsel of others, because God may use them to show you the way. Ask God to help, and then give thanks, because He will do it.

Hope

EXPECT THE BEST

*"I know the plans I have for you," declares
the L*ORD*, "plans to prosper you and not to
harm you, plans to give you hope and a future."*
JEREMIAH 29:11 NIV

Of God's many kindnesses to you, the gift of hope
strengthens you today and allows you to face tomorrow
with confidence and optimism. Your God-given hope,
unlike wishful thinking, is based on what He has done
for you already. He has brought you to this day and
blessed you greatly up to this point. Though you may
wonder how He could possibly use some of the things
that have happened to you for your good, He has in
the past, and He will in the future. Place your hope
firmly in Him, and expect the best—you'll get it!

REAL HOPE

You listen to the longings of those who suffer.
You offer them hope, and you pay
attention to their cries for help.
PSALM 10:17 CEV

When you're in despair, you need real hope. Platitudes don't work, and neither do assurances of a sunny tomorrow. Thank God for those kind and thoughtful people who can provide real reasons to hope! The words they say show that they're not afraid to walk beside you in your suffering. They're listening, and they're picking up on the depth of your feelings. The hope they extend to you is meaningful, fact-centered, and backed up by practical help whenever possible. They give you strength to move forward, the same thing you can give to those who look to you for hope.

Humility

HEART-DEEP HUMILITY

Toward the scorners he is scornful,
but to the humble he gives favor.
PROVERBS 3:34 ESV

Your aptitude for kindness depends on your attitude toward others. If, for example, a person looks down on others, she's unlikely to treat them with patience, tolerance, and compassion. But with a God-given humble heart, your capacity for kindness is limitless. You know yourself as an imperfect being, and so you readily forgive the shortcomings of others. You never boast about yourself but eagerly praise, support, and encourage the abilities and talents of others. Though you aren't looking for it, praise comes pouring back to you because genuine, heart-deep humility is at work in your life.

MEASURE OF GREATNESS

*"It is the one who is least among
you all who is the greatest."*
LUKE 9:48 NIV

Jesus, in His earthly ministry, paid special attention to those who were little valued at the time—widows, children, beggars, lepers, and the disabled. His example teaches all who follow Him that God looks not at outward appearances or attainments but at the heart. All too often He finds arrogance in the hearts of the socially privileged but humility, kindness, sincerity, and generosity in the hearts of those they look down on. No matter where you rank in society's eyes, the eyes that really matter see inside the heart. You might be surprised to discover who's the greatest!

Individuality

INCOMPARABLE YOU

God has given different gifts to each of us.
1 CORINTHIANS 7:7 CEV

You've heard it said, "Don't compare apples to oranges."
Though apples and oranges differ in appearance,
texture, and sweetness, both taste good. It's possible
you enjoy them equally! So when you compare yourself
to others, guess what you're doing? Comparing apples
to oranges. Your gifts, talents, and abilities are different than those of other people, and at the same time,
you're inferior to no one. Yes, let the positive attributes
and notable accomplishments of others inspire and
motivate you to do your best, but do not compare.
Do yourself a kindness and cherish the God-given,
incomparable you!

SINGULAR KINDNESS

*"Are not five sparrows sold for two pennies?
And not one of them is forgotten before God."*
Luke 12:6 esv

Say you're in a hot-air balloon hovering high over a packed football stadium. From that distance, you see no individual faces but only a mass of people crowded around a patch of turf. How differently God sees you! To Him, you are not one of a huge population but an individual created and loved by Him. There's no way He could ever forget about you or skip over you, any more than you would willfully forget, ignore, or neglect the people you love. To you, they are individuals that you regard with singular kindness, just the way God regards you.

Integrity

BEWARE OF SHORTCUTS

*What will you gain, if you own
the whole world but destroy yourself?*
MARK 8:36 CEV

In life as in driving, shortcuts can take you where you don't want to go. Promises of easy money, effortless achievement, and instant status most likely have an "if only" attached, and this "if only" is something that compromises your integrity. There's a price to pay, and it could be your honesty, reputation, principles, and self-respect. The next time you're tempted to take a shortcut, do yourself a kindness. Consult the One who wrote the map. Ask God where the road leads before you take it.

KINDNESS IN ALL CASES

*The integrity of the
upright will guide them.*
PROVERBS 11:3 NKJV

Many people practice kindness. Some do kind things when they feel the person deserves a good turn, or they have the time, or a convenient opportunity presents itself. For others, however, kindness is an aspect of integrity. They act kindly in all situations because kindness is one of their values. Since their self-respect demands kindness, they don't ask whether it's deserved or convenient to be kind; they just go ahead and act kindly. Isn't that a lot like God? And with His Spirit at work in your heart, it's a lot like you too!

Joy

LASTING JOY

The fruit of the Spirit is love, joy, peace.
GALATIANS 5:22 NKJV

There's a difference between happiness and joy. Happiness depends on how you feel and the circumstances around you. If you're feeling good and everything's going your way, you're happy, right? But there are days you're under the weather and things aren't working out at all. Not happy! By contrast, God-given joy is heart-deep, and it doesn't depend on anything except God's presence in your life. You trust in His goodness, rely on His kindness, and rest in His love. What could ever take away your joy?

PICTURE OF JOY

He helps me, and my heart is filled with joy.
I burst out in songs of thanksgiving.
PSALM 28:7 NLT

Joy and times of trouble don't seem to go together, but they do when joy is Spirit-born and Spirit-fed. When you're disappointed, take joy in remembering that God has good plans for you and will not let you down. When you're ill or injured, pray for His healing touch and joyfully leave the outcome in His loving hands. When you're undergoing any hardship, lean on His strength and be joyful because He knows, understands, and cares. Joy and times of trouble definitely go together when God is part of the picture.

Laughter

A GREAT KINDNESS

A joyful heart is good medicine.
PROVERBS 17:22 ESV

The greatest kindness you can do for others is to meet them right where they are. It might mean graciously celebrating a friend's promotion you had hoped would be yours, or patiently listening to a relative's woes. But sometimes meeting people right where they are is as small and simple as laughing with the child who tells you a joke you learned in kindergarten, with the friend who's amused at her own witticisms, with the coworker who delivers the funny line you've heard dozens of times before. Yes, laughter is a kindness, and a great kindness.

A LAUGHING MATTER

A time to weep and a time to laugh,
a time to mourn and a time to dance.

ECCLESIASTES 3:4 NIV

Some people burst out in laughter at anything, while others laugh at nothing. Neither extreme requires the effort of separating what's funny from what's not, nor honors God's gift of laughter. Godly laughter lights up your face, lifts your mood, and shares the glow of good feelings with everyone around you. It's kindly, well meant, respectful, and appropriate to the time, place, and people present. As you can imagine, godly laughter requires God-sent thought and Spirit-led discernment to know what is—and what is not—a laughing matter.

Leadership

SHOW OF LEADERSHIP

*"You should be a light for other people.
Live so that they will see the good things
you do and will praise your Father in heaven."*
MATTHEW 5:16 NCV

Even if you don't possess a title that identifies you as a leader, you still lead. The daily example you set in how you speak and the way you act influences others to follow you. If you let yourself fall into carelessness and negativity, you're giving vulnerable people an excuse to do the same thing. But if you're mindful of others, reflecting compassion and kindness in the things you say and do, you're showing people how to apply God's guidelines to everyday life. You're a leader! The only question remaining is "What kind of leader are you?"

A LASTING LEADER

"My sheep listen to my voice;
I know them, and they follow me."
JOHN 10:27 NIV

"Take me to your leader," the extraterrestrial says to the astonished human who discovers the UFO in his backyard. But consider this: What if your shadow gave you the same directive? Would you lead her to a political figure, a public speaker, a relative, a friend, your own thoughts and ideas, or God? If your leader is anything or anyone less than God, your leader is fallible, frail, and temporary. Such leaders lead for a time, but their power and influence eventually diminish. Take anyone—including yourself—to your lasting leader, who is God alone.

Learning

KEEP LEARNING

If you have good sense, instruction will help you to have even better sense. And if you live right, education will help you to know even more.
PROVERBS 9:9 CEV

Even given opportunity, contacts, and every push possible, you won't learn unless you're willing to learn. Some people will learn when they're small, but then they decide at a certain point that they know all they need to know. That's when they stop learning. Others reach a milestone age or particular level in their career, and they close their ears to any new information. That's when they stop learning. God's Spirit promotes lifelong learning. That's how He nurtures compassion, kindness, tenderness, understanding, and love in you. It just keeps growing as long as you're willing to keep learning.

A GOOD EDUCATION

*False teachers will also sneak
in and speak harmful lies to you.*
2 PETER 2:1 CEV

If you want a good education, it's important to choose a good teacher. You want someone who knows the subject, is able to teach others, and can answer your questions. For your spiritual learning, the same thing holds true. Pray that God will put you in contact with someone who knows God's Word, will speak His truth in love to you, and will challenge you to grow and increase in wisdom. Look for someone who teaches not only in words but also by example. Search until you find such a teacher, because your spiritual learning is for a lifetime—and beyond.

Life

SPIRITUAL LIFE

"The Spirit of God created me,
and the breath of the Almighty gave me life."
JOB 33:4 NCV

Though the formation of physical life can be explained in human terms, the creation of the soul remains a mystery. Your soul, your God-space, is a place God has reserved for Himself; yet because of His kindness toward you and His regard for you, He waits for you to invite Him in. One condition, though: He is willing to share this sacred space with no one else and with nothing else. Let His presence fill every corner of your heart, soul, and mind, and light every aspect of your life.

A MEANINGFUL LIFE

None of us lives for ourselves alone.
ROMANS 14:7 NIV

Though some claim that their life is their own to do with as they please, God says differently. He gave you the gift of life, and then He set down guidelines so you could live it fully and joyfully. In scripture—His instruction book for life—He invites you to live, not for yourself alone, but to bless others with your time and attention, your words of comfort and encouragement, your acts of kindness and compassion. Let God, the One who created life, show you the way to a life of meaning, purpose, and lasting joy.

Loneliness

COMFORT IN LONELINESS

I am the LORD your God, and I will
be there to help you wherever you go.
JOSHUA 1:9 CEV

Have you ever felt completely alone? Perhaps you moved far from family and friends, and you found yourself ill at ease among unfamiliar faces. Or you started a new job and had yet to get acquainted with your coworkers. Pangs of loneliness are sharp! Yet no matter where you are, God provides the comfort of His presence, a presence that soothes the ache of loneliness. Put your trust in His compassion, and open your eyes to the person He sends to offer you the kindness of a welcoming word, the warmth of understanding, and the hand of friendship.

THE FAMILY OF GOD

God sets the lonely in families.
PSALM 68:6 NIV

You belong to the family of God. In His family, you have countless mothers and fathers, sisters and brothers throughout the world, and you're related by faith to the women, men, and children who are part of your worship community. It's in this family that you'll find sisters and brothers to support and encourage you, as well as elders to share their experience with you, as well as young people who look to you for help and inspiration. Your spiritual family is another example of God's kindness to you and just another reason to share His kindness with one another.

Love

LOVE IS POSSIBLE

"If you love only the people who love you, you will get no reward."
MATTHEW 5:46 NCV

Loving people who love you is easy! They're kind and gracious to you, and you can depend on them to stand by you and be there whenever you need their help or advice. You can trust them to keep your confidences, defend your reputation, and care about your problems and concerns. But how about other people—those who are indifferent to you, even those who are unkind to you? God invites you to love them too. It's never easy, but His Spirit at work in your heart makes it possible for you to love everyone, even them.

MARKS OF LOVE

Don't just pretend to love others.
Really love them.
ROMANS 12:9 NLT

Genuine love for others isn't marked by warm and fuzzy feelings or a fleeting sense of oneness with the world. Quite the contrary! Even though genuine love emanates from God's Spirit living and working in your heart, its marks are obvious, objective, and evidenced in the things you do and say. The gentle words you use when you speak and the practical help you offer to those in need prove the presence of love. What's more, your daily faithfulness, loyalty, and dependability are all marks of genuine, God-inspired love.

Marriage

BRING BACK THE JOY

*Those who live in love live
in God, and God lives in them.*
1 JOHN 4:16 NCV

The bond of marriage provides countless ways to practice kindness. Yet all too often in the routine of day-to-day life, husbands and wives forget the small kindnesses and thoughtful gestures they showered on each other in the springtime of their romance. You don't need a time machine, however, to bring back some of the joy of first love. All it takes is a willingness to speak gently and act considerately today, and remain patient through times of hardship and trial. That's something your loving God does for you.

A SACRED TRUST

Give honor to marriage, and remain
faithful to one another in marriage.
HEBREWS 13:4 NLT

Whether you are married or single, you have a responsibility concerning marriage. Your marriage, along with the marriages of others, has been brought into existence through the solemn promises spoken by husband and wife. It is a sacred trust. You honor marriage when you do everything you can to support and encourage all married people to love, cherish, and remain faithful to each other. Speaking kindly about your husband and refusing to disrespect anyone's spouse are two ways you can fulfill your responsibility concerning marriage.

Opportunity

DAILY OPPORTUNITIES

Listen! I am standing and knocking at your door.
If you hear my voice and open the door,
I will come in and we will eat together.

REVELATION 3:20 CEV

No matter where you are in life or the circumstances surrounding you, God desires to enter your heart. Every day is an opportunity to meditate on His presence in your life, recall the many ways He has blessed you so far, and contemplate the kindness He has shown you by calling you His own. You have an opportunity to pray at any hour, knowing He will hear you and respond to your call. There's not a moment that goes by without a God-given opportunity to bask in His love for you.

PAY ATTENTION!

"Look, I tell you, lift up your eyes,
and see that the fields are white for harvest."
JOHN 4:35 ESV

God sends countless opportunities to you to practice kindness. Look with the eyes of your spirit and see those who need your prayers—a friend going through a tough time, an aging relative struggling with loss and limitations, the victims of the disaster that you have heard about. When you go out, yield to others rather than rush on ahead. Smile, acknowledging the presence of God in each person you meet. Pay attention, and you'll find plenty of small, seemingly inconsequential opportunities to practice kindness. Who knows, but one might be the best thing to happen in someone's day!

Past

REMEMBER YESTERDAY

Watch yourselves closely so that you do not forget the things your eyes have seen or let them fade from your heart as long as you live.

DEUTERONOMY 4:9 NIV

At times you may feel as if you're at a spiritual standstill. You can't see where God is working in your life and you haven't experienced His presence in quite a while. Why not do what His people have done throughout history? Remember how He has helped you in the past—the unexpected opportunities, narrow escapes, remarkable insights, out-of-nowhere courage and boldness when you needed it. He will do all those things for you again! Rest at ease; treat your soul kindly with the comfort of knowing you remain in His loving care.

A VIEW OF THE PAST

Think about past generations.
Ask your parents or any of your elders.
DEUTERONOMY 32:7 CEV

A good way to learn about recent history is to talk with someone who was there. You have the opportunity to hear how the events touched one person's life, and many older men and women take it as a compliment when you ask them about their past and listen to their story. Those ahead of you in your spiritual life have a story to tell too. They probably have been through many of the struggles you are going through now and would gladly share their thoughts and advice. Why not do them (and yourself) the kindness of asking?

Patience

THE RIGHT TIME

Lord, how long must I ask
for help and you ignore me?
HABAKKUK 1:2 NCV

"Lord, give me patience—*right now!*" Perhaps you can relate to the funny line because you're used to getting answers, information, and products you want quickly, if not instantly. But God doesn't work that way. Though technology and other innovations have considerably sped up many functions, God continues to set the pace of events. The change or development you yearn to see happen, the goal you can't wait to reach are on God's schedule. To you it might seem like a long time, but be patient. God alone knows the right time.

ESSENTIAL TRIO

Love is patient, love is kind.
1 CORINTHIANS 13:4 NIV

Love, patience, and kindness go together. In fact, it's hard to imagine love that would not express itself in both patience and kindness! That's because even intense, God-sent love for the people in your life does not protect you from feeling annoyed with them or exasperated by their actions from time to time. Yet true love prompts you to respond with patience, not intolerance, as they struggle through their weaknesses. True love compels you to treat them with kindness, not malice, when they upset or offend you. Love, patience, kindness—three must-haves for strong, healthy, and lasting relationships.

Peace

PEACE RESTORED

*God is not the author
of confusion but of peace.*
1 CORINTHIANS 14:33 NKJV

Disputes erupt in homes, churches, workplaces, and communities—wherever people gather. In the heat of the moment, hurtful words are hurled and lines are drawn between "for" and "against," "us" and "them." Who can restore peace? Perhaps you can. God's Spirit of peace empowers you to resist pressure to take sides and to discern the core issue and present it with clarity and consideration for the feelings of everyone involved. Remain full of God's peace, and you might be the one who restores peace with your understanding, kindheartedness, and God-sent wisdom.

TRUE PEACE

*Let the peace that comes
from Christ rule in your hearts.*
COLOSSIANS 3:15 NLT

You might have thought this: *If only things would be peaceful around me, I would feel at peace.* But why wait for a time that will never come? There are enough problems brewing and glitches looming to keep peace at bay for a long, long time! What God offers you is peace that does not depend on outside circumstances, but on Him. When He fills your heart with faith in His promises, reliance on His strength, and the certainty of His presence, you have peace—peace that frees you to live with serenity, gentleness, kindness, and joy at all times.

Perseverance

CONTINUE IN HIS WAY

*Let us not become weary in doing good,
for at the proper time we will reap
a harvest if we do not give up.*
GALATIANS 6:9 NIV

Sometimes you do someone a great favor, but the person doesn't even so much as thank you. You go out of your way to show warmth, kindness, and friendliness to a newcomer, but your efforts bring no more than a chilly nod. As slighted as you may feel, don't let the thoughtlessness of others change your kind and caring ways. Instead, forgive them, be patient with them, and pray that God would soften their hearts and open their eyes to the beauty of gentleness and the grace of a generous spirit. Persevere in the way of love, compassion, and kindness.

KEEP GOING

*We must be determined to
run the race that is ahead of us.*
HEBREWS 12:1 CEV

In any worthwhile endeavor, you face challenges. It might be the tediousness of practicing the same thing repeatedly until you master the movement, the difficulty of grasping a demanding subject, or the time it takes to gain experience and expertise in a particular field. Yet when you reach your goal, you celebrate your victory. Along your spiritual journey you will also face challenges. There will be times you don't feel as if you're making progress, or that you're further from God than when you started. But persevere! Keep going, because you will reach your goal—you have His Word on it.

Power

A MODEL OF POWER

For He spoke, and it was done;
He commanded, and it stood fast.
PSALM 33:9 NKJV

Wherever you hold power over others—family, workplace, church, community—you can use it to worsen or improve their condition, to enrich yourself or enhance the lives of those under your authority. Look to God for your model! By His power He created a world of infinite beauty, formed life in His divine image, and continues to treat His people with limitless kindness and compassion. That's how to handle power that never corrupts but enables His love to reach out, lift up, and do good. That's the power He has given to you.

POWER TO ACT

Do not withhold good from those to whom
it is due, when it is in your power to act.
PROVERBS 3:27 NIV

Good people will avoid committing intentional acts of cruelty or meanness against others. But what sometimes escapes attention are the acts of kindness that they could have done but didn't. Inattention, busyness, distraction, and carelessness combine to hide from you your God-given power to bless others with everything from a casual greeting to a helping hand in time of need. Let Him open the eyes of your spirit to the depth and breadth of the power He has given to you so that when there's a kindness to be done and you are able to do it, you will.

Praise

HEAR THE PRAISES

*They loved praise from people
more than praise from God.*
JOHN 12:43 NCV

Praise makes you feel good—it affirms what you're doing and lets you know that others notice and care. More important than the praise itself, though, is who is doing the praising. If your kudos are coming from those who disregard God's ways, that's a signal that you could be straying from His path. But if you're hearing choruses of "Good job!" and "Well done!" and "Thanks for your kindness!" from people who know and love God, then give thanks. You are an inspiration to everyone around you.

PRAISE HIM!

*You should praise the LORD for his love and
for the wonderful things he does for all of us.*
PSALM 107:8 CEV

When you pray, God invites you to ask for the
things you need and desire. In addition, He opens
His arms to the confession of your faults, and He promises His unconditional forgiveness for whatever
you bring to Him. Yet there's one thing lacking in
many prayers, and that's unbounded, heartfelt praise.
Today and every day, praise Him for the gift of life
and breath! Praise Him for your ability to think and
act according to His will for your life! Praise Him for
His many kindnesses toward you! Praise Him for the
privilege of showering His kindness on others.

Prayer

NOTHING ELSE WILL DO

*The LORD is near to all who call on him,
to all who call on him in truth.*
PSALM 145:18 ESV

Who can measure the many kindnesses of the Lord! His promise to hear, listen to, and answer your prayers is a stellar example of the love He has for you. By asking you to pray, He prompts you to clarify your thoughts and express your deepest desires. As you recall His nearness, He strengthens your trust in and reliance on His power in your life. When you say, "Your will be done," you're reminded of His good and gracious disposition toward you and His plan and purpose for your life. Why do anything else but pray for the journey?

ACCORDING TO HIS WILL

*"I will do whatever you ask in my name,
so that the Father may be glorified in the Son."*
JOHN 14:13 NIV

As you grow in your spiritual life, you begin to lose many of the attitudes and desires that once weighed you down. More and more, your focus turns to God and the principles and values that mark a life lived in His Spirit. You're no longer bound to self-made plans but open and accepting of what God has in mind. You're not dependent on what the world says you need; you rely on what God, in His overwhelming kindness, provides. Is it any wonder, then, that your prayers reflect His will? They do, and His answer is "Yes."

Presence of God

BECAUSE OF LOVE

"Can anyone hide from me in a secret place?
Am I not everywhere in all the heavens
and earth?" says the LORD.
JEREMIAH 23:24 NLT

Imagine you are a mother with a newborn infant. There's not one instant that you would want your infant out of your sight, because you know the little one is helpless without you. Her life depends on your kindness and care, and you shower her with your constant oversight and attention. Though this image reflects only a fraction of the love God has for you, it serves to explain why He insists on His presence in your life 24-7. He knows you better than you know yourself, and He's in your life because of His indestructible kindness and everlasting love.

THE DESIRE IS MUTUAL

I will walk with you—I will be your God,
and you will be my people.
LEVITICUS 26:12 CEV

Certainly your desire to walk closer with God is something to celebrate. Your willingness to learn more about His ways and to apply His principles to your life is cause for rejoicing, because now you can bless others with His comfort, forgiveness, kindness, mercy, and encouragement. You probably have experienced the satisfaction of knowingly and willingly doing His will many times already! But there's even more to celebrate, and that's God's desire to walk with you. His presence means it's going to be a purposeful, meaningful, and fruitful journey. Take delight in every God-sent step!

Priorities

FIRST THINGS FIRST

"Seek first God's kingdom and what God wants.
Then all your other needs will be met as well."
MATTHEW 6:33 NCV

Think about the things you do every day almost without fail. No matter how busy you are, you make time for the things that are truly important and meaningful to you, don't you? Yet setting aside daily time with God is often put off "until later" or "tomorrow," even though it's the most important and the most meaningful thing anyone can do. If this has been happening in your life, do yourself the ultimate kindness: put time with God first on your to-do list, and you'll be surprised how well the day proceeds!

RIGHT PRIORITIES

Pursue righteousness and a godly life, along
with faith, love, perseverance, and gentleness.
1 TIMOTHY 6:11 NLT

Actions make priorities clear. If someone's main concern is making money, she devotes her thoughts, time, and energy to the pursuit of money. Anyone can see what ranks first with her! But if her number-one priority is God and His will for her life, she'll take a different path. She'll devote her mental, emotional, physical, and material resources to applying God's teachings to real-life situations. Instead of focusing her eyes on herself, she'll look for ways to serve others with God's love, kindness, and compassion. Her priorities are evident and obvious—and spot-on.

Problems

USEFUL PROBLEMS

*We also have joy with our troubles, because we know
that these troubles produce patience. And patience
produces character, and character produces hope.*
ROMANS 5:3-4 NCV

Though problems aren't welcome, they show up anyway.
Big or small, however, problems can bring out the best
in you if you meet them not with fear but with firm
confidence in your God-given abilities and resources.
Perhaps a little ingenuity and creative thinking takes
care of relatively minor issues, and each time you're
successful, you're building the skills you need to tackle
major problems when they appear. Ask God to give you
the confidence you need to reach godly and practical
solutions to all your problems. And what better kindness could you do than help others solve theirs?

NOT A PROBLEM!

*The LORD is good, a stronghold
in the day of trouble.*
NAHUM 1:7 NKJV

God has never promised a problem-free life, but He has promised His help with any and all problems. No matter how the problem came about or how many times it has cropped up in your life, you can rely on His strength and wisdom to help you deal with it. If it's a problem that concerns you, it concerns God. Let God express His kindness toward you by allowing Him to hear whatever weighs on your mind, fully trusting that He listens, cares, and will help you find the right solution for you and those you love.

Protection

PROTECT AND BE PROTECTED

*Live under the protection of God Most High
and stay in the shadow of God All-Powerful.*
PSALM 91:1 CEV

Kindness compels you to protect those weaker than yourself. The time you take to ensure the safety of children, warn a fearful friend, or rescue an animal in distress is your kindness at work. Yet what you're doing is only a shadow of the protection that God, in His kindness, provides to you. He watches over your soul so you are able to withstand temptation and resist those things that would take you away from Him. He keeps you safe, gives you His guidelines, and rescues you when you're in trouble. You are protected now and always!

PROTECTION PROMISED

Fearing people is a dangerous trap,
but trusting the LORD means safety.
PROVERBS 29:25 NLT

From time to time a situation arises that confronts you with a choice: Compromise your God-given values of kindness, gentleness, and love to gain the approval of those around you, or side with God's guidelines and bear their condemnation. In theory it's easy to choose the latter, but in real-life circumstances you might not feel so sure. That's why God makes His pledge of protection clear. The threats of others or any consequences they may mete out are nothing compared to what God provides—courage, strength, compassion, understanding, and lasting peace of mind.

Purpose

THERE'S A PURPOSE

In Christ we were chosen to be God's people,
because from the very beginning God had
decided this in keeping with his plan.
EPHESIANS 1:11 NCV

It's not by chance that you are interested in drawing closer to God. In fact, before you had the capacity to even think about Him, He was thinking about you. The time and place you were born and the events of your life are part of His purpose for you. Though you may wonder why something happened or fail to see how it could possibly have played a part in the plan of a kind and loving God, He knows. Even if you can't understand His purpose for you right now, take heart, because He does.

GOD-GIVEN PURPOSE

*Whether you eat or drink, or whatever
you do, do all to the glory of God.*
1 CORINTHIANS 10:31 NKJV

When you think about your life's purpose, perhaps your thoughts go directly to a particular calling or momentous mission. More often than not, however, God puts things on a smaller, but no-less-important scale. He blesses you with day-to-day responsibilities that He intends for you to do with acceptance, gratitude, and joy. He puts you among people with the expectation that you will serve them with kindness and tenderness, patience and gentleness. And He has surrounded you with the magnificence of all creation. Purpose? For you to enjoy to the fullest!

Regret

NO REGRETS

Godly sorrow brings repentance that
leads to salvation and leaves no regret.
2 CORINTHIANS 7:10 NIV

If you have more than a few candles on your birthday cake, you're likely to harbor a measure of regret. You remember the time you could have helped but didn't, the time you said something better left unsaid, the time you failed to choose the wisest course of action. For all those times, your compassionate God accepts your heartfelt repentance and comforts you with His complete forgiveness. In kindness, He removes the burden of regret, strengthening your capacity to understand and willingness to forgive those who wrong you. No regrets! Only wisdom, maturity, and peace of mind.

WHAT IF?

Godliness with contentment
is great gain.
1 TIMOTHY 6:6 ESV

"What if?" is a question often loaded with regret. What if you had chosen a path other than the one you did? What if you were living there rather than here? But those "what ifs" only serve to take your attention away from what is, and it's where you are right now that God meets you. Not in speculation of what might have been, but in real life God opens opportunities for you to bless others with acts of kindness, gentleness, and love. There's no decision you have made that God can't use to prove His kindness, gentleness, and love for you.

Relationships

THE MOST IMPORTANT RELATIONSHIP

*Since we have been made right with
God by our faith, we have peace with God.
This happened through our Lord Jesus Christ.*
ROMANS 5:1 NCV

No other kindness in the world can match the kindness of Jesus Christ! Remaining God, He was born in human flesh specifically to fulfill God's promise to send a Savior into the world. This Savior would make it possible for all who believe to enjoy a firm, living, and vibrant relationship with God, a relationship open to you today. The kindness you show others and the selfless things you do for them will reflect the most important relationship in your life—the one with God that Jesus has made possible for you.

GODLY RELATIONSHIPS

Don't fool yourselves.
Bad friends will destroy you.
1 CORINTHIANS 15:33 CEV

The people you're around all day and the ones you see socially exert a profound influence on you. Even without your conscious consent you pick up their attitude and outlook, words and phrases. What they tell you enters your thoughts and often sways the choices you make. For these reasons, your relationships matter to you and to God. As much as possible, surround yourself with people who will encourage your godly values, walk with you in your spiritual journey, and support you in your desire to grow in kindness, tenderness, and love.

Renewal

A NEW DAY

"Look, I am making everything new!"
REVELATION 21:5 NLT

God's Spirit works in willing hearts. From natural self-centeredness, His Spirit instills compassion for those who suffer fear and distress, hurt and harm. He motivates kindness toward all, especially those who are weak and defenseless; and He inspires genuine gladness for the blessings God showers on whomever He pleases. God restores the repentant to relationship with Him through forgiveness and the assurance of His continued love and care. He renews His promises of kindness, tenderness, generosity, and understanding to you every new day.

SOUL'S RESTORATION

He restores my soul; He leads me in the
paths of righteousness for His name's sake.
PSALM 23:3 NKJV

From the depths of despair, it's hard to believe that
God will—or would want to—pick up the broken heart.
Yet He does! No place you can land is so low that
God cannot reach down to lift, restore, and renew the
soul that cries out to Him for help. If you are able to
confess your transgression, God is more than able to
forgive you, comfort you, and return you to a peaceful
and productive relationship with Him. For your sake
and for His sake, He offers and provides these great
kindnesses to you.

Respect

REASON FOR RESPECT

"I am the LORD; that is my name;
my glory I give to no other."
ISAIAH 42:8 ESV

Many people, even people of great distinction and achievement, shun titles and prefer to be called by their first names. They want to blend in with everyone else, and they seek no special consideration because of their status. Your God is much different. While He bends down to meet you, serves you, and cares for you like no other, He reserves the right to ask for your respect. He is the One who showers every blessing on you and holds ultimate authority over you. His overwhelming kindness toward you claims your deepest worship, honor, and respect at all times.

RESPECT FOR ALL

*"God has shown me that I should no longer
think of anyone as impure or unclean."*
ACTS 10:28 NLT

Not everyone behaves respectably or holds respect
for others. How easy and how natural it is to withhold
from them any thought of mercy or act of kindness! Yet
even the worst offender possesses a God-given soul.
No group of people lies outside the reach of God's
unconditional forgiveness and transforming Spirit.
Because you believe in Him, His love goes out to others
in the things you do and say, including the feelings you
harbor about specific groups and individuals. Let His
compassion move you to respect everyone as a God-
formed person, just like you.

Rest

REST AT EASE

*"Come to Me, all you who labor and
are heavy laden, and I will give you rest."*
MATTHEW 11:28 NKJV

God is compassionate. He understands the stresses and anxieties you face in your life. He knows your struggles, your fears, and the concerns that constantly weigh you down. But compassion means little without action, doesn't it? So God puts His compassion in motion by inviting you to bring your tired heart and mind to Him in prayer. Let yourself relax in the comfort of His love for you. Allow Him to lift your burdens from you; experience the freedom of knowing that He is there for you. Rest at ease in Him!

TRUE REST

Comfort, comfort my people, says your God.
ISAIAH 40:1 ESV

If you have someone in your life who is unfailingly kind toward you, you are blessed. In this person's presence you can relax, be yourself, and talk about your concerns without worrying that you'll be judged or criticized. When you're particularly stressed or fatigued, this person is the one you want to be with and talk to! A genuinely kind person offers rest for tired spirits and burdened hearts in a way no one else can. Give thanks for the kind people you know. And be blessed for all the times your kind ways have offered others soul-deep rest.

Reward

REWARDED FIRST

*You treat us with kindness and with honor,
never denying any good thing to those who live right.*
PSALM 84:11 CEV

Some people do the right thing because they're motivated by the promise of a reward. For every gesture of kindness or offer to help, they expect payment, whether in money, a favor in return, or praise in front of others. But your Spirit-inspired motivation is different. You do the right thing in response to the reward you already possess—your God-given heart of kindness and attitude of compassion. All you think, say, and do come in thanksgiving for the reward He has reserved for you from the very start—the reward of His love.

GOD-SENT REWARD

Whoever sows to please the Spirit,
from the Spirit will reap eternal life.
GALATIANS 6:8 NIV

Wherever Spirit-planted faith takes root, kindness follows. One alone isn't the real thing! Faith that doesn't express itself in observable and practical acts of kindness toward others can hardly be called genuine faith in a God of lively, active kindness. At the same time, kind acts not motivated by faith in God are rooted in human desire, which is apt to fade or change or seek gain in return. Nourish your faith in God so kindness will overflow in your life—and yes, there will come a reward. That's a God-sent promise.

Righteousness

THE RIGHTEOUS HEART

*What does the LORD require of you
but to do justice, and to love kindness,
and to walk humbly with your God?*
MICAH 6:8 ESV

Who would not long for a heart right with God? That's
what it means to be a righteous person. Yet when the
conversation turns to righteousness, the word is most
often applied to someone who has done a particularly
admirable and heroic act. Certainly notable acts of
honesty, kindness, and goodness are righteous, but so
are the much smaller, much less noticed, and completely
ordinary. When God's Spirit fills your heart, mind, and
soul with love for Him and love for people, you are
a righteous person performing righteous acts every
single day.

POWER TO RESPOND

If you suffer for doing right,
you are blessed.
1 PETER 3:14 NCV

When you live a righteous life, you draw people's attention. You stand out because you don't go along with the crowd or agree with popular opinion or approve what God has condemned. Your principled words and actions make people think, and some will turn against you, even mocking you or insulting your intelligence. Yet your commitment to God and His principles gives you strength, power, and willingness to respond with unfailing kindness to those who scorn you, further establishing you in a life of God-blessed righteousness.

Sacrifice

VICTORIOUS OUTCOME

"I am the good shepherd. The good shepherd gives His life for the sheep."
JOHN 10:11 NKJV

From the very beginning, God's plan of salvation centered on Jesus' sacrificial death on the cross and His victorious resurrection from the grave. Jesus' sacrificial act fulfilled every requirement; your faith in His sacrifice is all you need to gain God's favor! As your Savior, however, Jesus did something else: He showed you that when you sacrifice your time, effort, and resources on behalf of others, you're doing more than a few simple kindnesses. You're acting like your Lord, and the outcome of your sacrifice is victory.

IT'S NO SURPRISE

Do not forget to do good and to share with others, for with such sacrifices God is pleased.
HEBREWS 13:16 NIV

You might not imagine that the godly things you do are sacrifices on your part, but they are. Anytime you don't give in to anger or impatience, you're sacrificing your natural feelings and offering peace and forbearance instead. Whenever you meet unkindness with kindness, you sacrifice a very human reaction for God's reply to those who turn their backs on Him. God meets everyone with mercy, forgiveness, and blessing. All the sins of the world He answered with the sacrifice of His Son on the cross! It's no surprise that you don't think twice about making sacrifices for others.

Salvation

A REAL GIFT

"Believe in the Lord Jesus,
and you will be saved."
ACTS 16:31 NIV

A genuine gift doesn't cost you a cent. It's given to you because the giver loves you and wants to make you happy. Who would insult such a gracious person by pulling out money to pay for the gift? Yet that's what happens when godly acts are done to earn salvation! It's trying to pay for the gift of love God has given to you solely because He delights in you and desires to fill your heart with joy. Doing good—not to earn His gift but to thank Him for it—provides your Spirit-given motivation for your many kindnesses to others.

GOD IS SALVATION

"The Son of Man came to look for
and to save people who are lost."
LUKE 19:10 CEV

When someone you love turns away from God's path and spurns His love, you're sick at heart. It's like watching a person head into an overgrown forest without a map, compass, or provisions. But here's another picture: God Himself scouring that same forest looking for your loved one. When He hears a cry for help, He comes running. He will delve into the deepest cavern or climb the steepest precipice to rescue one soul. He will be their salvation. Pray! Remain open to their return with a heart of kindness, forgiveness, and understanding. That's exactly what God is doing.

Security

ALWAYS SECURE

Those who trust in the LORD are like Mount Zion,
which cannot be moved, but abides forever.
PSALM 125:1 ESV

In a world of uncertainty, security seems like a relic of a bygone era. But because God never changes, you can always feel secure in His presence, His protection, and His kindness toward you. In addition, you can provide others with the gift of security. Your faithfulness in loving, serving, and being there lets them know they can depend on you. They can trust you, secure in the knowledge that you have their best interests at heart and will never fail to stand by them in their time of need. Security isn't gone, but alive and well in every God-filled heart.

FULL SECURITY

"No person can steal my sheep
out of my Father's hand."
JOHN 10:29 NCV

Spirit-planted and Spirit-nurtured faith keeps you secure in God's loving embrace. Even if someone belittles the values and principles you know are godly and right, you have His strength to rely on. You possess His wisdom to defend your faith by telling the truth in the kindest possible way. Should your weaknesses or shortcomings move you from His grasp, His hands remain outstretched to welcome you right back again. Unless you want to get away, He won't let you go. Rest easy and secure in your relationship with Him!

Self-Control

REGAIN CONTROL

Control yourselves and be careful!
The devil, your enemy, goes around like
a roaring lion looking for someone to eat.
1 PETER 5:8 NCV

Bad choices morph into bad habits. Perhaps early on control is possible, but there comes a time when it's not. A bad habit takes one away from her responsibilities, compromises her health and well-being, prevents her from caring about others, and distances her from friends and family. But if she's a woman of faith, she has the power of God's Spirit to help her regain control of her life. He enables her to reach out to God and to those around her who can help. Pray for God's control over your life and the lives of those you love.

A HIGHER POWER

I want to do what is good, but I don't.
I don't want to do what is wrong,
but I do it anyway.
ROMANS 7:19 NLT

Out-of-control people aren't noted for their kindness! Just the opposite. Someone with a short fuse quickly loses control over thoughts and feelings, words and actions. Someone who won't control personal wants and desires quickly descends into a life of selfishness and greed. Though human emotions can run high, however, God's power is even higher—divinely higher! Pray for Him to bless you with His power to control your emotions and reactions so nothing stands between you and the ability to respond kindly to others, treat them with respect and gentleness, and enjoy serenity and peace of mind.

Service to God

BUSINESS AS USUAL

We are God's fellow workers.
1 CORINTHIANS 3:9 NKJV

Service to God sounds like a lofty ideal. In movies the decision to serve Him might be accompanied by expressive, stirring music. In real life, however, service to God is business as usual. It happens whenever you, because you love God, do a kindness for someone else. Perhaps fixing a child's lunch, visiting a hospitalized friend, checking in on a neighbor you haven't seen in a while. All those routine kindnesses you do for the sake of God are your service to God. Pretty humdrum, isn't it? But not to those blessed by your kindness and love!

THE HEART COUNTS

Now we serve God in a new way with the Spirit,
and not in the old way with written rules.
ROMANS 7:6 NCV

Imagine you are sitting in a restaurant. The waiter hands you the menu, takes your order, brings out your food, and gives you your check. Yet in all this time, she hasn't smiled once or done anything beyond the minimum requirements of her job. Clearly, her heart isn't in it. This is not the kind of service God desires from you. One kindness done with joy and enthusiasm ranks higher than several performed with indifference or out of obligation. With God, it's not simply what you do but how you do it that counts.

Simplicity

SIMPLE LOVE

The teaching of your word gives light,
so even the simple can understand.
PSALM 119:130 NLT

If a lecture isn't delivered with skill and clarity, you're going to leave the room scratching your head. You might even wonder if the subject is too difficult for you to comprehend. Then later, you make a discovery: the subject isn't hard to understand, but the presenter made it so. Many would-be leaders muddy spiritual matters with intricacies and complications, yet the message of God's love in Jesus is crystal clear. It's so simple that even young children can understand. God's unfailing kindness and compassion toward you and all His people has made it just that way.

SIMPLY SPIRITUAL

"All you need to say is simply 'Yes' or 'No';
anything beyond this comes from the evil one."
MATTHEW 5:37 NIV

Many people have found that giving up high-maintenance possessions and time-consuming pursuits simplifies their lives considerably. Now their days are freer and their activities more manageable. In the spiritual life too, simplicity proves a great benefit. By not striving to attain esoteric knowledge or extraordinary insights, you're free to focus on what really counts—loving God and serving the people around you. Simple faith, simple trust, simple kindness, and simple love are all it takes for a strong, vibrant, and purposeful spiritual life that you, by God's grace, can manage and enjoy every day.

Sleep

GET SOME SLEEP

Those who work hard sleep in peace.
ECCLESIASTES 5:12 NCV

If you're like most women, your days are packed. Though you're exhausted by evening, you're still busy seeing to the needs of the household and preparing for the next morning. Of course you know you need more sleep and you would love to have it, but it rarely happens. If this sounds all too familiar, do yourself a huge kindness. Find a workable way to get the sleep you need at least most nights. It matters to you because you'll feel better, to others because you'll serve them more joyfully, and to God because He delights to give you rest.

A WATCHFUL EYE

He who keeps Israel will
neither slumber nor sleep.
PSALM 121:4 ESV

When God doesn't answer prayer right away or He seems unconcerned about your concerns and problems, you might wonder if He isn't sound asleep! How can He not hear your cries? How could He not know your troubles? But His love for you and His kindly attitude toward you would never allow Him to turn away from you one moment, much less shut His eyes and doze off. During a hectic day, His calming presence remains with you. During even the darkest night, His watchful eyes protect you. Sleep in peace, because He knows, He cares, and He will help.

Speech

BONUS KINDNESS

*"Out of the abundance of the
heart the mouth speaks."*
MATTHEW 12:34 ESV

If you've ever inadvertently blurted out an ugly remark, you know the danger of harboring unkind thoughts. They don't remain thoughts forever! Sooner or later, the feelings, opinions, and judgments that occupy your heart make their way to your attitude and to your lips, and become clearly evident. To speak kind words to others, fill your heart with positive feelings, compassionate views, tender thoughts, and a gracious attitude toward everyone. That way, should you ever blurt something out, you won't have to worry—it will be a bonus kindness!

STRONG LANGUAGE

When you talk, you should always be kind and pleasant so you will be able to answer everyone in the way you should.
COLOSSIANS 4:6 NCV

It's called "strong" language—vulgarity, swearing, and expletives. Language with real and lasting strength, however, has nothing to do with offensive words. Truly strong language consists of words that inspire, empower, and encourage; words that create understanding, reveal compassion, and build community; words that possess precise meaning and informative value. These mighty words belittle no one but serve to uphold the dignity of all. They are kind words, even when their message is difficult to believe or uncomfortable to hear. When you speak, use strong language—the kind with real strength!

Spiritual Growth

SURE AND STEADY GROWTH

We will not be influenced by every new teaching we hear from people who are trying to fool us.
EPHESIANS 4:14 NCV

Fads in music, food, and fashion sweep the country, and suddenly it seems as if everyone is caught up in them. In faith matters also, fads pull many away from God-centered beliefs and biblically sound teachings with the promise of instant insights or quick rewards. Don't waste your time! For sure and steady spiritual growth, feed your faith with God's unchanging and nourishing Word. Let His Spirit deepen your understanding of all things spiritual at His pace and lead you along the way He has laid out ahead of you.

A WAY TO TELL

Run from temptations that capture young people.
Always do the right thing. Be faithful,
loving, and easy to get along with.
2 TIMOTHY 2:22 CEV

How spiritually mature are you? There's a way to tell, and that's how consistently you apply your spiritual knowledge and understanding to your daily circumstances. Think back on the past several days. Have you taken opportunities to show others kindness, especially now that you realize how important kindness is to true spiritual life? Have you remained calm and patient, even in those times you felt frazzled or stressed out? How about the things you've said and the tone of voice you've used? Let God's Spirit continue to show you many more ways to make your spiritual maturity show!

Spirituality

DAILY BREAD

"People do not live by bread alone; rather, we live by every word that comes from the mouth of the LORD."
DEUTERONOMY 8:3 NLT

If you were to buy a rose bush and plant it in good soil but never water it, the bush would not thrive for long. While you provided soil, you didn't provide water; the plant needs both. You too need two things to thrive: food for your body and food for your soul. Even if every physical need were met, you would still sense a lack in your life without your spiritual questions answered and your spiritual longings satisfied. Look to God's great kindness to provide your daily bread—the practical kind and the spiritual kind.

ACTION-PACKED SPIRITUALITY

*The mind governed by the
Spirit is life and peace.*
ROMANS 8:6 NIV

True spirituality is much more than a dreamy desire for oneness with God. Rather, it's action-packed and expresses itself in real-life circumstances. As God's Spirit continues to lead you on the spiritual path, observable changes take place in your life. For example, self-centered ambition gives way to God-centered goals and objectives. You notice who around you could use a little extra help or encouragement, and you give it. You're in a place where kindness and gentleness are in short supply, so you take it upon yourself to provide the warmth of friendliness, generosity, and goodwill. That's spirituality in action!

Strength

GOD'S HELPING HANDS

The LORD is my strength and song,
and He has become my salvation.
PSALM 118:14 NKJV

DIYers take notice: building a life of godly kindness isn't a do-it-yourself project! No one, without Spirit-planted power, has the strength of heart and mind to consistently resist the pull of selfishness and impatience. Not one person, without Spirit-sent sight, is able to perceive the real needs of others and meet them with God's love and compassion. That's why God promises to help you as you build more kindness, more gentleness, and more love into your thoughts and actions. He gives you the spiritual strength to do the God-pleasing things that you desire.

YOUR STRENGTH AND POWER

Where sin was powerful,
God's kindness was even more powerful.
ROMANS 5:20 CEV

The pull of temptation is strong—extremely strong! And the weight of guilt is powerful enough to crush even the most resilient spirit. God's love for you, however, comes on much stronger and much more powerfully than any force of darkness. His kind heart and compassionate feelings toward you compel Him to brace you against temptation, forgive you whenever you stumble, and shine the light of His wisdom and guidance ahead of you. You need never walk in the shadows or suffer under the weight of despair. Because of His kindness to you, you possess true strength and power.

Success

A MEASURE OF SUCCESS

*"Life is not measured
by how much you own."*
LUKE 12:15 NLT

You know how the world measures success—the more popularity, status, and stuff you possess, the more successful you are! As you can well imagine, God turns that definition on its head. Regardless of how much success in the eyes of the world you have (or lack), God looks at how your faith in Him is working in your life. He measures your success by the gentleness of your thoughts, the kindness of your words, and the helpfulness of your actions. While worldly success belongs to an individual, godly success radiates from heart to heart to heart.

ABOVE ALL SUCCESSES

*I have fought the good fight, I have
finished the race, I have kept the faith.*
2 TIMOTHY 4:7 ESV

Who doesn't want success in reaching goals, meeting objectives, and gaining the heart's desire? Indeed, God has a plan and purpose for you, and as you follow His path, you will be met with success after success. Yet one success rises above all others, and that's success in holding firmly to your faith in Him through every stage of life. If your faith wavers or even ebbs at times, God's Spirit stands ready and eager to fill you with renewed strength and confidence. You can depend on His great kindness, because He, more than anyone, wants you to succeed!

Thankfulness

SPIRITUALLY NATURAL

*Be thankful in all circumstances, for this is
God's will for you who belong to Christ Jesus.*
1 THESSALONIANS 5:18 NLT

It goes against human nature to give thanks while suffering bad circumstances! But because of His Spirit's action in your heart, gratitude is a gift available to you at all times, even times of hardship or misfortune. In less-than-favorable circumstances, thank Him for the comfort of knowing He is there for you, for the kindness of people who help and encourage you, for the experience and perspective you gain to understand others in similar situations. "Thank You, God" won't come naturally to your lips when you're going through tough times, but the words are likely to radiate from your Spirit-filled heart.

THANK YOU, GOD!

I praise you, LORD,
for answering my prayers.
PSALM 28:6 CEV

When you pray, think about all the blessings God has given to you, especially the ones He has showered on you this day. Let your words overflow with gratitude for the kindnesses you have received and the privilege of showing kindness to others. Nothing's too small to escape your notice! Mention the friendly chat with a neighbor, the warm smile of a passerby, or the helpful advice from a friend. Thank Him for the privilege of fixing dinner, connecting with a relative, praying for someone else's need. Thank Him for all the ways He has been super kind to you!

Thoughts

GOOD THOUGHTS

Keep your minds on whatever is true, pure, right, holy, friendly, and proper. Don't ever stop thinking about what is truly worthwhile and worthy of praise.
PHILIPPIANS 4:8 CEV

Not all notions that enter the mind are invited, or even appreciated. Disturbing thoughts are never welcome in a life devoted to peace and harmony, a relationship with God, and kindness toward others. Yet your spiritual progress depends on the kinds of thoughts that occupy your mind, because your thoughts inform and direct your actions. Let God's Spirit answer the door of your heart when unsettling ideas or suggestions come knocking. He has the power to push them away, leaving room for thoughts that please God, grant you tranquility, and benefit others—thoughts of kindness, goodwill, happiness, compassion, and love.

GOD'S GOOD THOUGHTS

*"My thoughts are nothing like your thoughts,"
says the LORD. "And my ways are far beyond
anything you could imagine."*
ISAIAH 55:8 NLT

No matter how spiritually minded you are, your human thoughts are but a dim reflection of God's thoughts. No one possesses the complete perfection of God's aims and desires, and not one mind can grasp the depth and breadth of God's great plan for the world and for every person who ever was, is, or will be in it. Now you know why His Spirit urges you to submit your thoughts to His, because God possesses authority over all things. Think—think thoughts of kindness, gentleness, truth, and affirmation—but humbly place them beneath the sublime understanding of your God.

LOOKING FOR MORE ENCOURAGEMENT FOR YOUR HEART?

Worry Less, Pray More

This purposeful devotional guide features 180 readings and prayers designed to help alleviate your worries as you learn to live in the peace of the Almighty God, who offers calm for your anxiety-filled soul.

Paperback / 978-1-68322-861-5 / $4.99

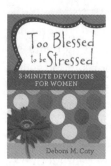

Too Blessed to be Stressed: 3-Minute Devotions for Women

You'll find the spiritual pick-me-up you need in *Too Blessed to be Stressed: 3-Minute Devotions for Women.* 180 uplifting readings from bestselling author Debora M. Coty pack a powerful dose of inspiration, encouragement, humor, and faith into just-right-sized readings for your busy schedule.

Paperback / 978-1-63409-569-3 / $4.99